Life is a Game

A COLLECTION OF POEMS

PRAGNA MANNAM

PARTRIDGE

To order additional copies of this book, contact
Partridge India
000 800 10062 62
orders.india@partridgepublishing.com

www.partridgepublishing.com/india

Life is a Game

CONTENTS

DEDICATION

I dedicate this book to my beloved grandparents.
They were consistently supportive of my writing
and encouraged me to follow my dreams.
I will always be grateful for their
compassion and guidance.

"Live as if you were to die tomorrow; learn as if you
were to live forever."
- Mahatma Gandhi

My grandparents, Dr. Amilineni Devarajulu Naidu, M.Sc, Ph.D and Amilineni Pramada Kumari, M.A, B.Ed who reside in Chittoor, India significantly encouraged my pursuit of higher education and the publication of my poetry. They have committed their lives to the excellence of education. My grandmother, who dedicated 42 years to education, is the recipient of several awards including Guru Brahma Award by Viswabharathy Academy and Eminent Educationalist Award. My grandfather, who is a retired professor in Chemistry, along with my grandmother established a private school serving K-12 in Chittoor, India. They received the Best School Award from the government of Andhra Pradesh in 2001.

ACKNOWLEDGMENTS

I would like to thank my parents for inspiring
me to reach my unrealized potential and
assisting me in the publication of this book.

I also want to acknowledge Soman Patnaik
for his beautiful and thoughtful illustrations
that integrate seamlessly into the poetry.

PREFACE

In our digitalized, highly technological world where the norm is frenetically hectic, Pragna Mannam invites you, through her poetry, to stop and reflect upon an appreciation of life. She captures the essence of our experiences, our challenges, and our innermost thoughts. Her messages which cover beginnings and endings, and our emotions and relationships in between, transcend all ages and resonate with all people.

Pragna Mannam is a multifaceted, extraordinarily talented young woman, who displays remarkable insight about human nature. She is the recipient of several national computer science and robotics awards, in addition to her extensive commitment to numerous volunteer endeavors, field hockey and Indian dance. She is currently attending Carnegie Mellon University in Pittsburgh, Pennsylvania.

Pragna Mannam's beautiful compilation of poetry, written during her school and college years, delights the senses, tantalizes the mind, and provokes deep contemplation.

Marilyn P. Maledon, Attorney

LIFE IS A GAME

Where the start is birth
And game over when the player leaves the board,
It is inevitable that you pass other players
And that many may surpass you.
Nevertheless, the extra mile is always less crowded.

There will be wrong turns and mishaps,
Built paths and new paths.
Where the worst of moves
Is to remove yourself from the board
And give up.

For there is no direction except forward
And no penalty except failure.
But failure is only a stepping stone
And success is your paradise.

Regardless of what situation you encounter,
Persevere and see
That only the players and the games are different.
But the principles are the same.

DEAR GRANDPARENTS

You showed me what to do,
You showed me how to tie a shoe,
And you showered me with love.

You taught me how to eat,
You taught me how *not* to eat,
And you told me how life works.

Now standing in two tied shoes,
I can tell you two,
That I couldn't have done it without you.

You taught me the importance of laugh,
The value of family and love,
And the reason to keep going.

I love you,
I miss you,
I hope you do
Miss me too.
I'm a poet
And I didn't even know it
Until you told me to just go for it.

A grandparent's love is irreplaceable,
And you've molded me while shapeable.
I have no regrets
And only hope
That you also find the same.

I have begun to walk the path
That you can turn around
And see for miles.

With your guidance,
I hope for the chance
To be the shining star
And the best I can be.

I love you,
I miss you,
And I wish you all the best.
I thank you for all you've done
And will love you forever more.

BLUE'S CLUES

When you are feeling down,
The world has ceased spinning around.
Something is terribly wrong.
It has been this way for too long.
It is the world vs. *you.*
You are feeling blue.
It seems like from everyone
You want nothing but to run.
There is nowhere else to hide
With too many problems to set aside.

When you think you are all alone,
There is more to it than shown.
Your betrayers and enemies are a mere number
That your family and loved ones completely outnumber.
Don't forget that there is more;
Keep swimming until you reach the shore
Because nothing else can stop you
Unless you do.

Life is difficult,

Smiles are an uncommon result.

But without those wide grins,

All you can see are the deep, dark sins.

The world would seem dreary,

Everything would be too eerie,

And life would just not be fun,

Without more than one pun.

Forget the troubles,

And drown yourself in the bubbles,

Of love and happiness.

Bask in glory by Jove!

Live to the fullest,

However blessed,

And enjoy every moment.

LIVING

I never understood.
I never analyzed.
I never knew
The true meaning
Of living life.
I thought it was simple:
Eat, breath, sleep.
To live every moment,
To not waste a second,
I thought,
I thought I knew
How to live,
And what to do.
Turns out there is more.
Much more.
The sorrow, pain, troubles,
That came along
For the ride called life.
The easy path it traveled on
Guaranteed a bumpy ride
With ditches and hills.
Ones which were unavoidable,
Inevitable,
And impacting.

Could it be that living,

was just enjoying life,

Whenever possible,

At every moment?

Or was it to experience sorrow

And only embrace happiness,

From the world around us

That provided all?

And now I can return

Something too.

To the world of the living,

I can say,

That what happens

Is something only time can tell.

But *you* can experience.

SPRING

Truthfully spring,
But the reality of winter.
The sun jumps into the sky,
Extending its rays farther than the ground.
Although the ball of heat appeared,
The cool breeze remains.
Walking outside,
Sniffles and sneezes are heard.
Soon enough the clouds claim the sun,
Rain pelts the earth,
Rebounding off the ground.

Maybe it is true to the calendar after all.
If this is spring,
I wonder what summer is.

Putting a spring in another's step could put one in your own.

LIGHT

The light bounces off the walls,
Like my spirit,
Never seen,
But always present.
Feeling bright and happy,
In the dark.
But swamped by others,
In the light,
Insignificant and nominal,
Fading away,
Never detected,
But alive.

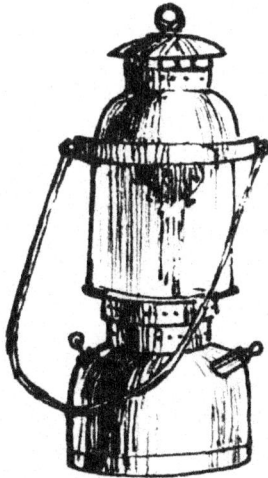

You cannot enjoy the calm unless there is a storm.

STORM

Everything sways from side to side,
From every leaf to every branch,
One raindrop lands on a flower,
Another follows.
The gap between each droplet closing,
The water weakens the wood,
The creak from stress amplifying,
One foot after the other.

The curtains are drawn,
Eyes gaze out,
The sky darkening,
The grass greener,
Droplets make ripples,
In the puddles on the sidewalk,
Rain pelting the trees.

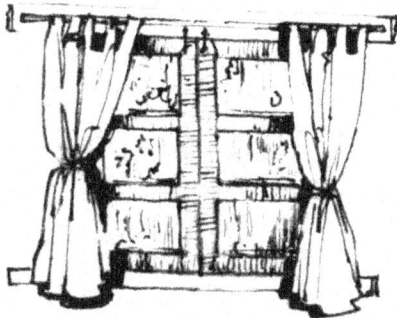

Afar a light is seen,
The bolt of electricity I presume.
Soon follows the booming sound,
Of the ever so late thunder,
The house's light flickers.

Eyes drift away from the window,
Everything is dark,
Besides the blazing flame,
Of a candlelight.

TALENT

Talent

Do I have any?

I think again and again,

And can't seem to find it.

Touched the keys of the grand piano,

Felt the void in my fingers a month later,

Saw the yellow ball bounce across the court,

A year later the racket is abandoned in the garage.

Driving to dance class years later,

I look out the window,

I remember that I haven't seen the

rectangular room in ages.

How will I find it? Does it exist? Within

my soul? Or lost forever?

A dream is like a cloud; you know how it looks but up close it is barely tangible.

DREAMS

Everyone has one,
Whether during REM,
Or as their daily motivation,
Something to drag them through everyday.

For better or for worse,
Aspiring to be,
Worth something,
The best at something,
Beating everyone,
Being worthwhile,
And useful,
The path seems stronger,
And brighter than ever.

Out of all of them,

One always seem better,

The one you have chased,

For what seems like an eternity.

But once in a while,

You get the eerie feeling,

That maybe it's wrong,

And there's a better choice.

But how will it be found,

And pursued,

For many paths grow blurry,

The brightest one fading.

In the distance,

You see,

Nothing but dark,

But later,

The dark ones turn to light.

SISTER GRADUATE

When we were younger,
We fought in the summer,
And almost every season after,
Especially because I thought I was better.

I'm sorry if I ever hurt you,
Now I wish you fought me back too.
You are the best sibling I could ask for,
Not that I have any more.

You always gave me advice on anything,
And yelled at me when I lost your ring.
We had the best and worst times,
And you never judged me. Well maybe sometimes.

You tolerated my craziness,
And my constantly changing obsessions.
I couldn't ask for more,
Well, maybe if you just didn't
always drag me to the store.
You've come a far way,
And now you're going so far away.

Be sure to enjoy your college life,
I know high school was a strife.
But that's the past now.
Somehow.

I have always idolized you,
I know you wish for me to surpass you too,
But I'm happy with just being your sister,
Or even just on par.
Because you are just that great,
And I have one last message if it's not too late:
Study, party, and stay on track.
Do your best and don't hold back.

Supporting you is a very loving family,

So don't ever feel lonely.

Keep moving forward,

And set your own record.

Live every moment to the fullest.

I love you and I'll miss you. I wish you the best.

There could be miles between you and home but only you can put the real distance between the two.

HOME

The path curved around the houses,
The gray sidewalk engulfed in bright green grass,
Identical houses line up along the sidewalk,
Bikes and scooters fill the silence of springtime,
Silent birds hum in the distance,
The leaves drifting away from tall brown trees,
Landing softly whichever way they are carried,
For the wind is their guide,
And the tree is their home.

We spend our lives fighting against time and wishing it wasn't finite, yet we procrastinate and lose the time we truly cherish.

PROCRASTINATION

The pile increases,
Reaching for the ceiling,
Never shortening,
But always lengthening,
Collecting higher and higher.
Like the dust on old photo albums,
I continue to watch it,
And then proceed,
To walk away,
And ignore it,
Once again.

When the deadline approaches,

Like the edge of the cliff,

I look out to the ocean,

The gentle waves,

Everything but the edge I stand on,

Because the pile is too large.

But in the end,

I only hurt myself.

AT HOME ALONE

Farewells fade away,
An engine roars,
Soon enough the car speeds away,
A voice cheers in silence,
Footsteps wander into the kitchen,
Junk food in hand,
The television turned on,
Slowly munching away,
Time passes,
And there goes the day,
With your fleeting freedom.

Indulge your future self through the actions of your present self.

THINGS TO DO

Too many things to do,
Too many to begin,
Too many to end,
Nowhere to start,
Only to fret,
About what to pick,
And what to do,
Sometimes there is too much,
And sometimes,
There's too less,
Where is the middle?
Where is the balance?
Between the two extremes,
Where am I?

Heads and tails, heat and cold, and light and dark. Each one needs the other and we need them both.

ABSENCE OF LIGHT

Darkness envelops the trees' green leaves,
Hiding the strong bark along with
the creatures of the night,
Swooping from place to place,
Lights disappear gradually,
Window to window,
And door to door,
As the end begins,
And introduces a new path.
Even as it seems dark,
It is only the absence of light,
But it may not always be so.

It's hard to live in the present, but if we aren't living in the past or future, then there's no other choice.

DEATH

It stalks, it creeps, it attacks.
From the first cry,
To junior high.
Anytime.

It stalks, it creeps, it attacks.
While on the job,
Around the globe,
Wherever.

It stalks, it creeps, it attacks.
Watching grandchildren play,
Laughing worries of old age away.
It is imminent.

It stalks, it creeps, it attacks.
One sudden day,
The lifeless body lay.
Game over.

It stalks, it creeps, it attacks.
But it lingers more.
The soul mourned for,
Cherished, forever.

If you are too focused on what went wrong, you will never see what went right.

SEVEN AGES OF WOMAN

The world is a stage,

And life has its acts,

Like the stages of a person's life.

First, you're an infant,

Crawling and dragging yourself,

Across the smooth wood floor,

Being carried by others,

And embracing all the hugs and kisses.

Then, you enter school.
You do your best to please your teachers,
And get what you want,
You make friends your age,
And you have no worries.

Later, you become a teen,
You try to fit in with the crowd,
Trying to be popular,
Throwing parties to make friends,
With finals and exams,
There's no way to avoid stress.
You go to dances and parties,
Flipping your hair when there's a guy around.

Later, you find the one meant for you.
You marry him and soon you're a wife.
You are scared of the commitment,
But later glad you made it.

You find a job.
You may hate it,
But it gets you where you need to be in life.

Then, you have a child,
Who you love with all your heart.
You spend all your time with the child,
And have a great time.
As the children grow older,
They start to leave home,
Flying off to another place,
Far, far away.

You are in middle-age now.
And it's just you and your husband,
Close to retirement.

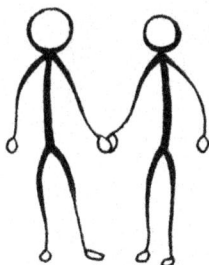

You think of things you've always wanted to do,
Because now you have the time,
To do anything.

Finally, you become a grandmother.
You spend all your time buying them gifts,

You play and pamper them,
And as time passes away,
So do you.

ABOUT THE AUTHOR

Pragna Mannam was born in Stoke-on-Trent, England and raised in New Jersey and Pennsylvania, U.S.A. She is studying Electrical and Computer Engineering at Carnegie Mellon University in Pittsburgh, Pennsylvania. She anticipates receiving her B.S. degree in May 2017.

Pragna has served as a Research Assistant in the University's Robotics Institute Manipulation Lab and a Teaching and Resident Assistant for a FIRST Robotics Competition Boot Camp. She is an Executive Member of the Society of Women Engineers at Carnegie Mellon University.

Pragna enjoys photography and writing poetry, which she has done since she was 12 years old. She is the daughter of Dr. Sudhakar Mannam and Dr. Padmaja Mannam. Pragna's sister Harshitha is a medical student at Northwestern University. The family resides in Pittsburgh, Pennsylvania.

CPSIA information can be obtained at www.ICGtesting.com
Printed in the USA
BVOW06s1324260716

456809BV00006B/29/P